American Moments

ABDO
Daughters

APOLLO 13
By Alan Pierce

VISIT US AT
WWW.ABDOPUB.COM

Published by ABDO Publishing Company, 4940 Viking Drive, Suite 622, Edina, Minnesota 55435. Copyright © 2005 by Abdo Consulting Group, Inc. International copyrights reserved in all countries. No part of this book may be reproduced in any form without written permission from the publisher. ABDO & Daughters™ is a trademark and logo of ABDO Publishing Company.

Printed in the United States.

Edited by: Melanie A. Howard
Interior Production and Design: Terry Dunham Incorporated
Cover Design: Mighty Media
Photos: AP/Wide World, Corbis, NASA

Library of Congress Cataloging-in-Publication Data

Pierce, Alan 1966-
    Apollo 13 / Alan Pierce.
        p. cm. -- (American moments)
    Includes index.
    ISBN 1-59197-726-6
    1. Apollo 13 (Spacecraft)--Accidents--Juvenile literature. 2. Space vehicle accidents--United States--Juvenile literature. I. Title. II. Series

TL789.8.U6A5685 2005
629.45'4--dc22
                                                        2004052982

CONTENTS

"HOUSTON, WE'VE HAD A PROBLEM"

On April 13, 1970, a U.S. spacecraft called *Apollo 13* rushed toward the moon. Inside were three astronauts, James A. Lovell, Fred W. Haise Jr., and John L. Swigert Jr. The astronauts were going to land on the moon to explore the hilly region known as the Fra Mauro range.

So far, the flight had gone smoothly. The astronauts had even filmed a tour of *Apollo 13* for news broadcasts. However, soon after the filming, a problem arose. A yellow light inside the spacecraft indicated possible trouble with the system that cooled the oxygen

James A. Lovell

Fred W. Haise Jr.

John L. Swigert Jr.

and hydrogen tanks. Mission Control in Houston, Texas, had monitored the problem and radioed instructions to stir the tanks.

A fan inside each tank did the actual stirring. Swigert turned on the fans to stir the tanks. Seconds later, an explosion shook the craft. Emergency lights began to flash and an alarm went off in Haise's headphones.

Swigert contacted Mission Control. "Hey, we've got a problem here." Mission Control asked the astronauts to repeat the message. Lovell replied, "Houston, we've had a problem."

The crew, indeed, had a problem. An oxygen tank had exploded while *Apollo 13* was 200,000 miles (321,869 km) from Earth. The loss of the tank endangered the astronauts because it provided them with some of the oxygen they needed to breathe. *Apollo 13* had also lost electrical power. The accident meant the astronauts would not be

Apollo 13 *blasts off inside a Saturn V rocket.*

landing on the moon. But no one knew if the damaged spacecraft could return to Earth. And no one knew if the astronauts would survive the journey home.

COLD WAR

The astronauts aboard *Apollo 13* had been heading toward the moon as part of a scientific expedition. But there was another reason for the flight. The Apollo program had been formed to show the supremacy of the United States over the Soviet Union. Since the end of World War II, the two countries had competed for dominance in the world. This rivalry was known as the Cold War.

Part of the conflict between the two nations sprang from their different political and economic systems. Americans practice a democratic form of government. They hold elections to choose leaders among different political parties. For its economic system, the United States relies on capitalism. Individuals and corporations own most of the goods. Also, businesses are encouraged to compete with each other to sell products and services.

In contrast, a different political and economic system existed in the Soviet Union. The Communist Party held all the power. This also meant that the Communist government controlled the economy.

These different outlooks made the Soviet Union and the United States view each other as enemies. The United States opposed Soviet efforts to spread Communism. Although the two nations were hostile, they wanted to avoid a war. Both countries had nuclear weapons, and a war between the two nations risked the destruction of both countries.

A replica of Sputnik

Technology was one area where the United States and the Soviet Union competed. Both countries wanted to show that their political systems produced the best technology. One way to demonstrate excellence in technology was to display leadership in space exploration.

On October 4, 1957, the Soviets began the space race by launching the first satellite into space. The 184-pound (83-kg) satellite was named *Sputnik*. It had a huge impact on the Cold War. After the satellite launch, it appeared that the Soviets had a head start in technology.

The United States responded to *Sputnik* by forming the National Aeronautics and Space Administration (NASA) in 1958. This agency was given the task of developing spacecraft and exploring space. The experienced personnel of the National Advisory Committee for Aeronautics (NACA) helped form NASA. NACA had conducted much of the advanced research in aviation in the United States.

In October 1958, the United States started Project Mercury. This project aimed to send humans into space to orbit Earth. In addition, the project would study the effects that space had on humans. The next year, NASA chose seven men to train to be the United States's first astronauts.

NASA logo

Despite Project Mercury, the Soviet Union continued to lead the United States in space exploration. On April 12, 1961, Soviet cosmonaut Yury Gagarin became the first man to fly into space. He orbited Earth once in the *Vostok 1* spacecraft. His flight made him a Soviet hero, and he became popular throughout the world.

Meanwhile, the United States suffered another setback in its struggle against Communism. This reversal occurred in Cuba, which is 90 miles (145 km) from Florida. A revolutionary leader named Fidel Castro overthrew Cuba's dictator, Fulgencio Batista y Zaldívar. Castro also became a dictator, but he formed an alliance with the Soviet Union. The U.S. government was upset about the presence of a Soviet ally so close to the United States. Soon, the United States plotted to overthrow Castro's Communist government. The plan called for exiled Cubans who opposed Castro to invade the island.

On April 15, 1961, Castro's enemies began bombing Cuban air bases. Cubans trained by the United States landed at the Bay of Pigs in southern Cuba on April 17. It was a disaster. Castro's forces quickly defeated the invaders and captured most of them. The attack became known as the Bay of Pigs invasion.

The United States, however, soon had an event to celebrate. On May 5, 1961, Alan B. Shepard Jr. became the first U.S. astronaut in space. He made his historic flight in the spacecraft *Freedom 7*. But Shepard's flight was less impressive than Gagarin's achievement. Gagarin had flown for 1 hour and 29 minutes to an altitude of 187 miles (301 km). Shepard's flight lasted 15 minutes and reached an altitude of 115 miles (185 km). The United States still lagged behind its Communist rival, the Soviet Union.

CUBAN MISSILE CRISIS

Nikita Khrushchev

U.S. and Soviet forces never fought a war with each other during the Cold War. But they came close. While both countries were deeply involved in the space race, one of the most serious conflicts of the Cold War occurred. This conflict also involved Cuba, and became known as the Cuban missile crisis.

In May 1960, Soviet premier Nikita Khrushchev promised that the Soviet Union would defend its ally, Cuba. In July 1962, the Soviet Union had begun to ship nuclear missiles to Cuba. By October 14, the United States knew that missile sites were being built on the island.

President John F. Kennedy was alarmed by this news. He felt that these missiles threatened the United States's role as a world power. But he was also afraid of responding to the missiles in a way that would plunge the world into nuclear war. On October 22, he announced that the United States would blockade Cuba and seize any missiles that the Soviet Union tried to ship there.

On October 24, Khrushchev warned that the Soviet Union would defend itself from U.S. "piracy." But soon, Khrushchev offered to remove the missiles from Cuba. However, he wanted the United States to promise not to invade the island. The United States agreed. Kennedy also secretly agreed to remove U.S. nuclear weapons from Turkey. Khrushchev ordered that the missile sites in Cuba be destroyed on October 28, 1962. This ended the Cuban missile crisis.

MERCURY, GEMINI, AND APOLLO

President John F. Kennedy wanted to propose a goal that would help the United States eclipse the Soviet Union. Furthermore, the president wanted to achieve this goal in space. He asked Vice President Lyndon B. Johnson to consult with leaders in NASA, industry, and the military. Many leaders favored a plan to land an astronaut on the moon.

On May 25, 1961, Kennedy delivered what became known as the Urgent National Needs speech to the U.S. Congress. During this speech, he announced a bold goal. "I believe this nation should commit itself, before this decade is out, to landing a man on the moon and returning him safely to this Earth. No single space project . . . will be more exciting, or more impressive to mankind, or more important . . . and none will be so difficult or expensive to accomplish."

After Kennedy's speech, NASA became committed to landing astronauts on the moon. On November 28, 1961, the agency awarded a contract to North American Aviation to develop the Apollo spacecraft. This spacecraft would be designed to take astronauts to the moon, land them, and bring them back to Earth.

NASA also began to achieve better results with Project Mercury. On February 20, 1962, John H. Glenn became the first American to

*In an address to Congress, President John F. Kennedy
makes landing an astronaut on the moon a national priority.*

orbit Earth. He completed three orbits in the spacecraft *Friendship* 7
before landing in the Atlantic Ocean. Project Mercury ended in May
1963, when L. Gordon Cooper Jr. completed 22 orbits in *Faith* 7.
By the time the project ended, U.S. astronauts had completed six
manned spaceflights.

President Kennedy did not live to see further U.S. accomplishments
in space. He was assassinated on November 22, 1963, in Dallas, Texas.
Vice President Johnson became president. He had helped pass laws to
create NASA. However, Johnson soon became distracted by many
problems facing the country. He did not always provide strong
leadership for NASA.

A Saturn V rocket on display at Johnson Space Center in Houston, Texas

After Project Mercury, NASA wanted to test its ability to guide and dock spacecraft. These skills would be important in reaching the moon. To this end, NASA started the Gemini program. In December 1965, *Gemini* 6 performed a successful rendezvous with *Gemini* 7 in space.

Project Mercury and the Gemini program had prepared the way to land astronauts on the moon. The challenge of fulfilling this goal was left to the Apollo program. This project developed the spacecraft and staged the missions that would lead to the moon landings.

NASA would require an incredibly powerful rocket to launch the Apollo spacecraft into space. The space agency designed the Saturn V rocket to do this task. The Saturn V stood 363 feet (111 m) high. It weighed 6.4 million pounds (2.9 million kg) when loaded with its fuel of kerosene and liquid oxygen. This fuel allowed the rocket to produce 7.5 million pounds (3.4 million kg) of thrust to escape Earth's gravity.

The spacecraft itself was made up of three main units: the command module, the service module, and the lunar module. The command module served as the control center for the Apollo spacecraft. It provided 210 cubic feet (6 cu m) of space for three astronauts. Moreover, the command module was pressurized. The astronauts did not need to wear space suits inside the capsule.

For most of the mission, the command module would be attached to the service module. This part of the spacecraft contained the oxygen supply for the crew. The service module also contained the electrical power system and computer system for navigation.

The lunar module was the only part of the spacecraft that would land on the moon. Two astronauts would descend to the moon in the lunar module while the third astronaut orbited the moon in the command module. At the end of the moon exploration, the astronauts would use the lunar module to return to the command module. The lunar module, like the command module, was pressurized.

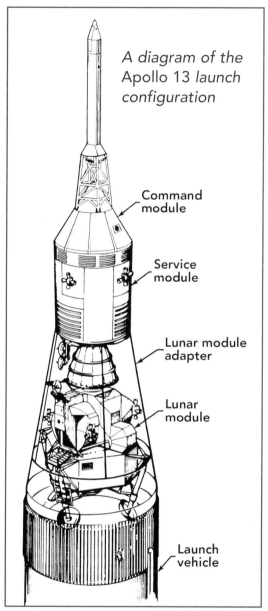

A diagram of the Apollo 13 launch configuration

Command module

Service module

Lunar module adapter

Lunar module

Launch vehicle

TRAGEDY AND TRIUMPH

On January 27, 1967, NASA planned a test at Kennedy Space Center in Florida. The test was a rehearsal for the countdown to liftoff. Astronauts Roger B. Chaffee, Virgil I. Grissom, and Edward H. White II took their places inside the command module as part of the exercise.

They practiced the launch inside a capsule that had been pressurized with pure oxygen. This environment was dangerous because oxygen is highly flammable. However, the Mercury and Gemini modules had also been filled with pure oxygen.

At 6:31 PM, a fire erupted in the command module. "Fire! We've got fire in the cockpit!" Chaffee yelled. The astronauts battled to escape from the capsule. But the hatch was difficult to open even under normal conditions. For more than five minutes, smoke and heat prevented NASA personnel from opening the hatch. They were too late. Chaffee, Grissom, and White had died. Later, NASA designated the test as the Apollo 1 mission, as a tribute to the three astronauts.

A NASA investigation concluded that an electrical spark had started the fire in the capsule. In turn, the pure oxygen in the capsule fueled the fire. The findings led to several changes in the Apollo spacecraft. Pure oxygen was no longer used in the module. Also, the later capsules featured a hatch that was easier to open.

Edward H. White II

Edward White was a West Point graduate and a lieutenant colonel in the U.S. Air Force. NASA assigned him to an astronaut team in 1962. White piloted the Gemini 4 mission in June 1965. For this mission, he earned the NASA Exceptional Service Medal and the U.S. Air Force Senior Astronaut wings. He was later named as a pilot for the Apollo missions.

Virgil I. Grissom

Virgil Grissom attained the rank of lieutenant colonel in the U.S. Air Force. He became a test pilot in 1955. In 1959, NASA selected Grissom to be one of the seven Mercury astronauts. On July 21, 1961, he piloted the Liberty Bell 7 Mercury spacecraft for 15 minutes and 37 seconds. Grissom later served as the command pilot on the first manned Gemini mission in March 1965.

Roger B. Chaffee

Roger Chaffee was a lieutenant commander in the U.S. Navy. He served as a safety officer and a quality control officer at the Naval Air Station in Jackson, Florida. Chaffee logged more than 2,300 hours of flight time. NASA selected Chaffee to be an astronaut in October 1963. He was chosen as a pilot for the Apollo 1 mission in 1966.

By late 1968, NASA was again ready for manned flight. On October 11, *Apollo 7* blasted off for an 11-day mission in space. This was a test to make sure the command module could function for an entire moon mission. NASA was concerned about the complicated commande module. But the module performed well during the successful mission.

In December, NASA launched *Apollo 8* while under intense pressure. There were still concerns that the Soviet Union might beat the United States to the moon. The Apollo 8 mission, however, marked an important milestone in the program. On this mission, astronauts made the first manned orbit around the moon. Lovell was part of the crew that achieved this historic feat. He piloted the command module.

Apollo 9 followed in March 1969. The purpose of this 10-day mission was to practice the maneuvers that would make a moon landing possible. Astronauts docked, separated, and performed a rendezvous with the command module and lunar module. In addition, astronaut Russell L. Schweickart tested the space suit outside the spacecraft.

On May 18, 1969, *Apollo 10* roared off toward the moon. This mission rehearsed the lunar landing without actually landing. The lunar module passed within 50,000 feet (15,240 m) of the moon's surface. Astronauts Thomas P. Stafford and Eugene A. Cernan reported good landing spots in the Sea of Tranquility.

NASA was ready to fulfill President Kennedy's goal of landing an astronaut on the moon in the 1960s. The astronauts slated to carry out this mission were Neil Armstrong, Edwin "Buzz" Aldrin, and Michael Collins.

On July 16, 1969, more than half a million people gathered near the Kennedy Space Center to watch the launch of *Apollo 11*. Millions of people around the world watched the event on television. Most sensed the excitement and historical significance of the mission. At 9:32 AM, the gigantic Saturn V rocket blasted off, taking *Apollo 11* and the three astronauts into space.

The flight to the moon went as planned. However, the landing of the lunar module *Eagle* was full of suspense. The *Eagle*'s guidance system threatened to land the module in a rocky area that would ruin the craft. Armstrong took over the piloting system to land the module

Michael Collins

Neil Armstrong

Buzz Aldrin

safely. He radioed back to Mission Control. "Houston, Tranquility Base here. The *Eagle* has landed."

A little later, Armstrong put on his space suit and set foot on the moon. As he did so, he spoke some of the most famous words in history. "That's one small step for man, one giant leap for mankind." Armstrong and Aldrin placed an American flag on the moon. There was no doubt that the United States now led the Soviet Union in the space race.

But the moon mission had risen above the Cold War. For many people, the moon landing demonstrated the best of what humanity could achieve. Armstrong, Aldrin, and Collins capped the mission with a successful splashdown in the Pacific Ocean. The new U.S. president, Richard M. Nixon, welcomed the astronauts when the crew returned to Earth.

NASA followed up Apollo 11 with a second moon landing, Apollo 12. This mission encountered problems immediately after liftoff on November 14, 1969. Lightning struck the Saturn V. Alarm lights lit up in the command module. However, Mission Control mastered the situation, and the mission continued flawlessly.

NASA had achieved two historic triumphs with the successes of Apollo 11 and Apollo 12. But already public interest in the manned lunar missions was beginning to fade. The space agency also received a smaller budget, which forced NASA to make hard decisions. NASA administrator Tom Paine decided to postpone the production of more Saturn V rockets. In January 1970, he canceled the Apollo 20 mission. The Apollo 13 mission, however, was still scheduled to journey to the moon.

Buzz Aldrin walks on the moon.

APOLLO 13

Like earlier Apollo spacecraft, *Apollo 13* was made up of three modules. It had a lunar module, a command module, and a service module. The lunar module was named *Aquarius*. The command module was known as *Odyssey*.

NASA had chosen Lovell, Haise, and Thomas K. Mattingly II to fly the spacecraft. Lovell would command the flight. Haise was the pilot of the lunar module. And Mattingly was assigned to pilot the command module. Mattingly was later replaced by backup crew member John L. Swigert. The crew had been exposed to German measles, and NASA thought Mattingly might not be immune.

With the three-man crew in place, the mission continued on schedule. On April 11, 1970, a Saturn V rocket blasted off from Cape Canaveral in Florida. The rocket carried *Apollo 13* and the three astronauts away from Earth. At first, the flight went smoothly. Mission Control updated the astronauts about baseball scores and events in the news. One of the technicians even told the astronauts that the people at Mission Control were bored.

By April 13, the mission was going well. Mission Control requested that the oxygen tanks be stirred. Swigert turned on the fans to stir the tanks. An explosion rocked the spacecraft 55 hours, 54 minutes, and 53 seconds into the mission. The blast occurred at

James A. Lovell

Jim Lovell was born
on March 25, 1928
in Cleveland, Ohio.
He attended the
University of Wisconsin,
and later received a
Bachelor of Science
degree from the U.S.
Naval Academy. Lovell
became an astronaut in
September 1962. In
December 1965, he and
astronaut Frank Borman
performed the first in-
space rendezvous during
the Gemini 7 mission.

John L. Swigert Jr.

John Swigert was born
in Denver, Colorado,
on August 30, 1931.
He attended the
University of Colorado
where he received a
Bachelor of Science
degree in mechanical
engineering. Before
becoming an astronaut,
Swigert served in the
U.S. Air Force. He also
served in the
Massachusetts and
Connecticut air
national guards.

Fred W. Haise Jr.

On November 14, 1933,
Fred Haise was born
in Biloxi, Mississippi.
He graduated from the
University of Oklahoma
in 1959, and began
serving as a research
pilot for NASA that
September. Haise wrote
several scientific papers
about spaceflight while
working for NASA.
In 1966, NASA selected
Haise and 18 others
to be astronauts for
the space program.

9:07 PM, Houston time. The astronauts thought a meteor had struck the spacecraft. Even a tiny meteor could cause major damage.

Soon, the astronauts and Mission Control began to see disturbing readings from their instruments. One oxygen tank appeared to be empty. Two of the three fuel cells were also dead. Lovell realized the moon landing might be cancelled. One fuel cell might provide enough power for the mission. But NASA insisted that all three fuel cells must function for a moon landing to proceed.

Meanwhile, the spacecraft was weaving out of control. Lovell struggled with the manual controls in the command module to bring *Apollo 13* in line. Despite his efforts, the spacecraft continued to veer off course. Lovell gazed out a side window to see if he could get a better sense of the problem. An awful sight appeared. A cloud of white gas surrounded the craft. Lovell told Mission Control that the spacecraft was venting gas into space. Mission Control suspected that *Apollo 13* was releasing oxygen.

There was more bad news. The instruments showed that the other large oxygen tank in the service module was slowly losing oxygen. When this oxygen was exhausted, the crew would have a small tank of

CAPE CANAVERAL

The Apollo spacecraft lifted off from
Launch Complex 39 at Cape Canaveral, Florida.

On November 28, 1963, six days after President Kennedy was assassinated, President Johnson made a televised address. He told the public that Cape Canaveral, Florida, would have its name changed to Cape Kennedy. This change would honor the slain president and recognize Kennedy's contribution to the space program. The name change took place in December.

Florida residents, however, were unhappy with the change. The cape had been called Canaveral for 400 years. For ten years, Florida tried to get Congress to change Cape Kennedy's name back to Cape Canaveral. When that failed, Florida's governor, Rueben Askew, signed an order to have Cape Kennedy renamed Cape Canaveral on May 18, 1973. The cape's name was changed on all State of Florida maps and documents.

In October, the U.S. Board of Geographic Names officially recognized the name change from Cape Kennedy to Cape Canaveral. John F. Kennedy Space Center, however, kept Kennedy's name.

oxygen left. This supply would keep them alive for only a few hours.

Lovell now realized that the crew must abandon *Odyssey* and board the lunar module *Aquarius* if they hoped to return to Earth. *Aquarius* was undamaged, but other challenges existed. The lunar module was designed to support two people for 45 hours. It now would be required to support three people for about 90 hours.

Mission Control had reached the same conclusion about the lunar module. Jack Robert Lousma of Mission Control suggested using the lunar module as a lifeboat to return to Earth. The crew agreed.

A model of the lunar module

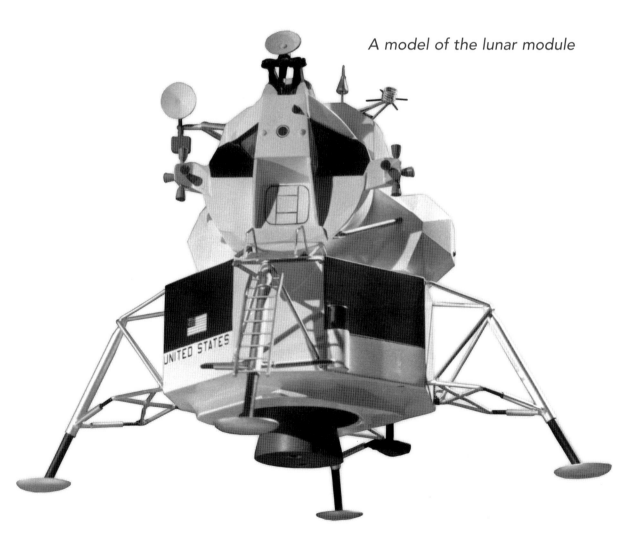

Tension is high at Mission Control in Houston, Texas, during the final 24 hours of the Apollo 13 mission.

Swigert shut off *Odyssey*'s systems to save its remaining power. The craft would still be needed for reentry. Lovell and Haise began to power up the lunar module. By 10:50 PM Houston time, the crew had abandoned *Odyssey*.

Meanwhile, more people were learning about NASA's emergency. NASA officials had contacted Lovell's wife, Marilyn, about the accident. She learned that *Apollo 13* was returning to Earth without landing on the Moon. However, astronaut Charles Conrad Jr. told her that the accident was very serious. By then, television stations had begun to report the accident. Marilyn watched as a correspondent reported that the astronauts had a 10 percent chance of surviving.

"YOU'VE GOT TO BELIEVE"

The odds were slim that the astronauts would return alive. But NASA was working to beat those odds. One of the first concerns was to get *Apollo 13* on the correct path home. NASA had a couple of options. One plan called for firing the powerful service module engine to stop the spacecraft and turn *Apollo 13* around toward Earth. But this idea had a weakness. After the accident, NASA officials did not trust the engine of the damaged service module.

Another option called for using the moon's gravity to hurl *Apollo 13* to Earth. This method required the spacecraft to swing behind the moon and then use the lunar module engine to adjust its course toward Earth. The lunar module engines had never been used this way. NASA lead flight director Gene Kranz decided to use this option. Mission Control informed the *Apollo 13* crew about the plan.

The trajectory of *Apollo 13* was not the only worry. Kranz was also anxious about the crew's limited supply of water, oxygen, and power. He formed the Tiger Team of 15 people to find solutions to these problems. Kranz gave the team its orders and then demanded that they be positive. "You've got to believe, you people have got to believe, that this crew is coming home."

While the Tiger Team labored to find answers, the crew also worked toward making progress. Early on April 14, Lovell fired

The Apollo 13 astronauts took this picture of the damaged service module in space.

Aquarius's engine for several seconds to set the spacecraft on the right course to sweep around the moon. The action was a success. NASA reported that *Apollo 13* was on the right path.

The *Apollo 13* crew needed some good news. Conditions inside the lunar module were miserable. The three men were cramped inside *Aquarius*. In addition, the interior of *Aquarius* was chilly. It had been 58 degrees Fahrenheit, (14°C) but the temperature continued to drop. The crew took turns trying to sleep in *Odyssey*. But *Odyssey* also was cold, and the men got little sleep.

Apollo 13 would get even colder when NASA's experts devised a plan to conserve power in the spacecraft. Mission Control told the astronauts to shut down most of the systems that used electrical power in the spacecraft. Among these systems was the cabin heater. Moreover, these electrical systems generated some heat, which would be lost when they were turned off.

The astronauts also had to conserve water. Their limited supply was needed both for drinking and for cooling the spacecraft's systems. In order to save water, the astronauts only drank about 6 ounces (177 ml) each day. This is about one-sixth the amount that an adult normally drinks. This meant that in addition to being cold and tired, the astronauts were also dehydrated.

At 6:15 PM April 14, Houston time, the spacecraft began to circle around the moon. For about 20 minutes, *Apollo 13* hurtled above the

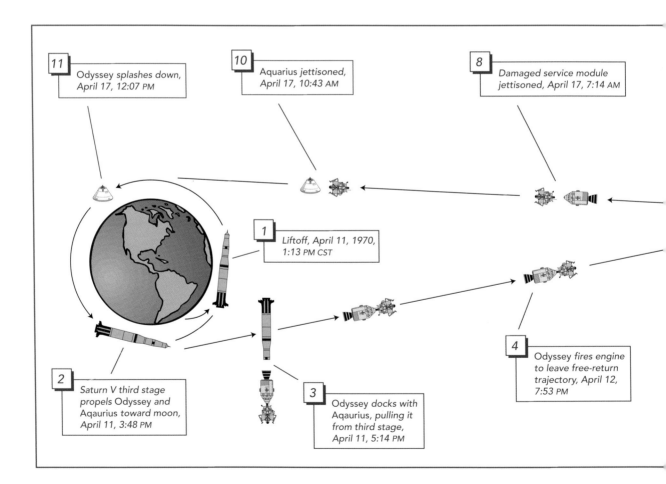

11   *Odyssey* splashes down, April 17, 12:07 PM

10   *Aquarius* jettisoned, April 17, 10:43 AM

8   Damaged service module jettisoned, April 17, 7:14 AM

1   Liftoff, April 11, 1970, 1:13 PM CST

4   *Odyssey* fires engine to leave free-return trajectory, April 12, 7:53 PM

2   Saturn V third stage propels *Odyssey* and *Aqaurius* toward moon, April 11, 3:48 PM

3   *Odyssey* docks with *Aqaurius*, pulling it from third stage, April 11, 5:14 PM

dark side of the moon. The astronauts wouldn't land on the moon, but they achieved another feat. They had traveled farther from Earth than any other humans.

Two hours later, the crew ignited *Aquarius*'s engine for five minutes. NASA hoped the acceleration would speed up the journey to Earth. The engine thrust also helped NASA calculate where the astronauts would splash down. NASA predicted that Lovell, Haise, and Swigert would return to Earth on April 17. The splashdown was to happen about 600 miles (966 km) southeast of American Samoa in the Pacific Ocean.

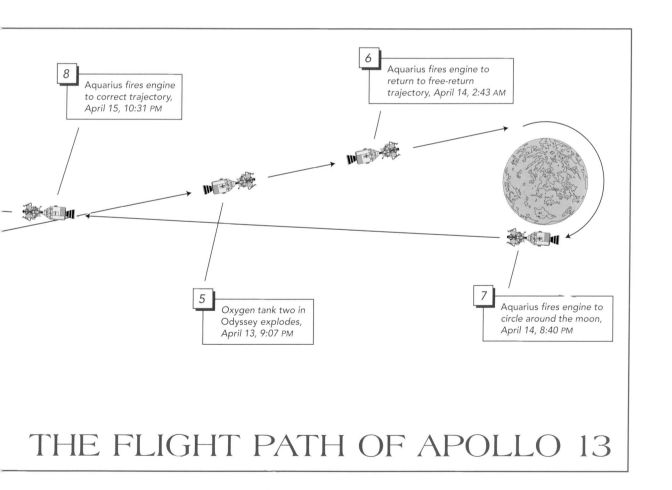

8 Aquarius *fires engine to correct trajectory, April 15, 10:31 PM*

6 Aquarius *fires engine to return to free-return trajectory, April 14, 2:43 AM*

5 *Oxygen tank two in Odyssey explodes, April 13, 9:07 PM*

7 Aquarius *fires engine to circle around the moon, April 14, 8:40 PM*

THE FLIGHT PATH OF APOLLO 13

SUCCESSFUL FAILURE

Apollo 13 was heading home. But the astronauts were still in danger. Although they had plenty of oxygen in *Aquarius*, they would eventually lose the ability to filter this air. The astronauts used lithium hydroxide cartridges to purify the air on *Aquarius*. These cartridges filtered out poisonous carbon dioxide. If most of the carbon dioxide could not be filtered out, the astronauts would die.

The astronauts had plenty of cartridges to filter the air. However, the cartridges from the *Odyssey* would not fit in *Aquarius*'s air-purification system. NASA estimated that the astronauts would run out of usable air by April 15. This was well before the April 17 splashdown.

NASA engineer Ed Smylie believed the cartridges from *Odyssey* could still be used. The astronauts would need to use materials aboard the spacecraft to make these cartridges work. Smylie tested his idea April 14, and the next day NASA informed the astronauts about the idea to use the cartridges. By this time, carbon dioxide levels in *Aquarius* had begun to increase.

NASA radioed instructions to the crew for constructing the adapter to the air-purification system. The plan called for using a plastic bag, cardboard, a sock, and duct tape to build an adapter.

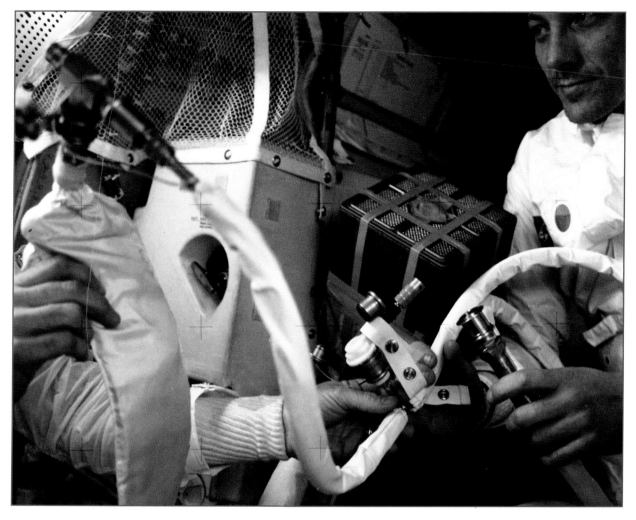

The Apollo 13 *astronauts assemble the converted air filter.*

The plan worked. Carbon dioxide levels in *Aquarius* dropped to acceptable levels.

Even with the oxygen problem taken care of, NASA and the *Apollo 13* crew still faced an enormous challenge. They needed to power up the command module. Only the *Odyssey* was designed to return to Earth. But starting up the command module was a tremendous undertaking. Because of the explosion, the checklist that NASA wrote for powering up the command module would no longer work. NASA had only three days to write a new one.

By April 16, NASA had produced a new checklist. However, by then drops of condensation had formed inside *Odyssey*. Condensation also covered the instrument panel. Lovell feared that the moisture might have damaged the command module's electrical equipment.

On April 17, Swigert and Haise began powering up the command module. No electrical problems occurred. Soon, the command module was up and running.

Next, the crew prepared the spacecraft for reentry. At 7:14 AM, the crew jettisoned the service module. The astronauts finally got a good look at the damaged craft as it floated away. They saw that one panel of the service module had been ripped away. The inside of the craft was exposed. Lovell saw that oxygen tank two was missing.

More than two hours later, *Apollo 13* cast off the lunar module. At Mission Control, capsule communicator Joe Kerwin paid his respects to the craft that had saved the crew. "Farewell, *Aquarius*, and we thank you."

At 11:53 AM *Odyssey* began its reentry. The friction with Earth's atmosphere would create temperatures of 5,000 degrees Fahrenheit (2,760 °C) on *Odyssey*'s heat shield. This intense heat also disrupted radio contact between the crew and Mission Control. This interference was expected. After four minutes, Kerwin attempted contact with *Odyssey*. For 80 seconds there was no response. Finally, Swigert responded. At 12:07 PM, *Odyssey* splashed down in the Pacific Ocean near the aircraft carrier USS *Iwo Jima*.

NASA failed to land *Apollo 13* on the moon. However, the agency had rescued the astronauts. The mission came to be known as a "successful failure."

SPLASHDOWN

After splashdown, a helicopter transported the Apollo 13 astronauts from the Odyssey command module to the USS Iwo Jima. The module was then recovered by U.S. Navy divers. In the photo on the right, Odyssey is being hoisted onto the Iwo Jima. The outside of the module looks like it is peeling. This is because of atmospheric friction during reentry. When a spacecraft enters Earth's atmosphere, it encounters friction as it speeds through the air. This friction causes intense heat, which could destroy the spacecraft if it were not protected.

The splashdown of the Apollo 13 command module in the Pacific Ocean

MISTAKES AND CONSEQUENCES

After the successful return of the astronauts, NASA concentrated on learning what caused the accident. NASA needed to do this before another Apollo mission could be launched. From photographs of the mangled service module, NASA officials did not think that a meteor had struck the module.

In order to study the matter further, NASA formed the Cortright Commission. It was led by Edgar M. Cortright. He was director of NASA's Langley Research Center in Hampton, Virginia. The commission studied the accident for three months.

The commission determined that improper switches in the oxygen tanks' thermostat had led to the explosion. In 1965, NASA engineers had changed the electrical system of the Apollo spacecraft from 28 volts to 65 volts. Each of *Apollo 13*'s oxygen tanks contained a fan, a heating element, and a shutoff switch that would turn everything off if the temperature inside the tank rose above 77 degrees Fahrenheit degrees (25°C). None of these had been redesigned to accommodate the increased voltage.

In addition, one of the tanks had been previously installed on *Apollo 10*. On the day it was removed, technicians dropped it. It was later fixed, then installed on *Apollo 13*.

A diagram of the inside of the Apollo 13 *service module*

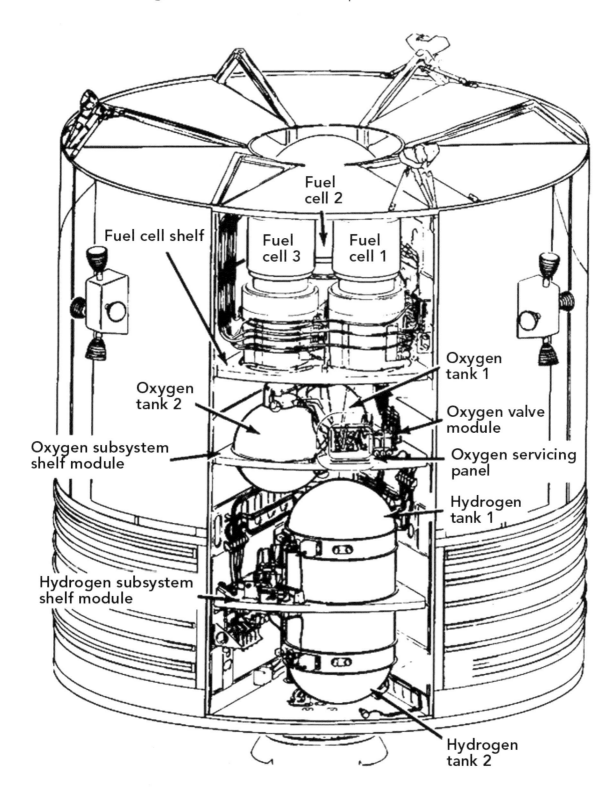

Fuel cell 2

Fuel cell shelf

Fuel cell 3

Fuel cell 1

Oxygen tank 1

Oxygen tank 2

Oxygen valve module

Oxygen subsystem shelf module

Oxygen servicing panel

Hydrogen tank 1

Hydrogen subsystem shelf module

Hydrogen tank 2

A pre launch check on *Apollo 13* showed the repaired tank from *Apollo 10* had trouble draining. But officials decided it would drain all right during the mission. NASA engineers turned on the heaters in the tanks to warm the oxygen enough to move the oxygen through a vent line.

But the switch, which was not designed for the 65-volt system, welded itself shut. Consequently, the thermostat failed to work. It did not indicate that temperatures inside the tank rose to 1,000 degrees Fahrenheit (538 °C). This intense heat burned away the Teflon insulation protecting the wires inside the tank.

Later, the tank was filled with oxygen for the mission. During the mission, the fan went on and the wires sparked. Then, the damaged Teflon insulation caught fire. The oxygen began to boil, and pressure inside the tank increased. The tank exploded and caused the other tank to leak its supply of oxygen.

NASA made some changes after the accident. The oxygen tanks were redesigned and another tank was placed in the service module. Furthermore, a backup battery was installed in the spacecraft for emergencies.

The accident had negative effects, too. President Nixon's advisers were worried that another accident in the space program could weaken support for the president. Space programs were already losing political support. The missions were expensive. Eventually, the entire Apollo project would cost the United States $25 billion. A smaller budget compelled NASA to cancel Apollo 18 and Apollo 19.

These decisions were setbacks for the Apollo program. But the misfortune of Apollo 13 did not end the moon missions. Apollo 14 was still scheduled to be launched in January 1971. The mission's original destination was near the Littrow crater in the Sea of Serenity. *Apollo 13*'s accident changed NASA's plans. *Apollo 14*'s landing site was changed to Fra Mauro.

The next Apollo missions were designed to allow the astronauts to spend more time on the moon's surface. In order to accomplish this, NASA built a Lunar Roving Vehicle to increase the distance the astronauts could travel. The rover was often compared to a dune buggy. It weighed 460 pounds (209 kg) and could travel up to 8 mph (13 km/h).

Eugene A. Cernan drives the Lunar Roving Vehicle on the moon.

Apollo 15 was the first mission to use the rover. This mission was launched on July 26, 1971, and reached the moon's surface four days later. During the course of three days, the astronauts drove the rover more than 15 miles (24 km) on the moon's surface.

On January 5, 1972, President Nixon announced a new direction for NASA. The space agency would focus on building a space shuttle capable of making as many as 100 flights. This would make space travel cheaper because an entirely new booster system would not be needed for each mission.

Nixon's announcement about the space shuttle program did not mean the Apollo program was finished. Two more missions remained. *Apollo 16* blasted off for the moon on April 16, 1972. The astronauts transported a special camera to the moon. This piece of equipment was called a far-ultraviolet camera/spectroscope. It recorded images of the ultraviolet spectrum, which cannot be seen with the human eye. Astronaut John W. Young used the camera to take pictures of Earth, nebulae, and star clouds.

The last mission in the program, Apollo 17, raised the public's interest again in moon landings. An estimated half a million people gathered at Cape Canaveral to watch the liftoff on December 7, 1972. This launch was even more spectacular because it happened at night. A night launch was necessary to time the mission so that the astronauts would have the best lighting conditions when they landed in the Taurus-Littrow area.

Apollo 17 also marked another milestone for the program. For the first time, one of the astronauts was a professional scientist. Astronaut Harrison H. Schmitt was a geologist, who had worked on mapping the moon. After training as a pilot and astronaut, he was

Schmitt (left), Evans (right), and Cernan (seated), pose for a crew photograph. The mission insignia appears above on the left.

selected to join the Apollo 17 mission. Geology played a large role in planning the mission. NASA wanted to search for evidence of volcanic activity on the moon.

Eugene A. Cernan commanded the final manned Apollo mission. The command module named *America* was piloted by Ronald E. Evans. On the mission's last day, Cernan spoke these words before he became the last man in the Apollo program to walk on the moon: "And as we leave Taurus-Littrow, we leave as we came in, and, God willing, as we shall return, with peace and hope for all mankind." On December 19, 1972, the manned lunar missions ended when *America* splashed down in the Pacific Ocean.

THE GREATNESS OF APOLLO

As the manned flights to the moon ended, NASA proceeded with its next undertaking. The Skylab project gave the United States its first space station. Skylab weighed almost 100 tons (91 t) and provided 13,000 cubic feet (368 cu m) of livable space for the astronauts. One of Skylab's main goals was to see if humans could live in space for long periods of time.

The Apollo program helped make Skylab possible. For example, the Saturn V rocket launched the massive Skylab into space. Also, the Apollo program had trained the astronauts who worked on the space station. Veterans of the moon landings such as Charles Conrad and Alan Bean lived, worked, and carried out experiments on Skylab.

The space station achieved one of its most important goals for NASA. Skylab showed that humans could live a long time in space. In fact, the last crew to visit Skylab lived 84 days on the space station. But after 1974, no astronauts lived aboard Skylab. On July 11, 1979, Skylab's debris crashed into the Indian Ocean and western Australia.

Later, the Apollo program came to be viewed as the peak of NASA's achievement. The moon missions are widely considered some of the greatest technological undertakings in history. In comparison to the triumphs of the moon landings, the Apollo 13 mission might seem like a disappointment. After all, it was considered a successful failure. But for the people at Mission Control, Apollo 13 was a victory. NASA had demonstrated that its experts could overcome long, terrible odds to bring its astronauts home.

Skylab orbits Earth.

TIMELINE

1957 On October 4, the Soviet Union launches the satellite *Sputnik*.

1958 The National Aeronautics and Space Administration (NASA) is formed and Project Mercury begins.

1961 On April 12, Yury Gagarin becomes first person in space. He orbits Earth in *Vostok 1*.

A U.S.-supported invasion of Cuba fails at the Bay of Pigs on April 17.

On May 5, Alan B. Shepard Jr. pilots *Freedom* 7, making him the first American in space.

President John F. Kennedy announces his goal to land man on the moon in his "Urgent National Needs" speech to Congress on May 25.

1962 On February 20, John H. Glenn becomes the first American to orbit Earth.

1967   On January 27, the Apollo 1 tragedy kills astronauts Roger B. Chaffee, Virgil I. Grissom, and Edward H. White II.

1968   On October 11, *Apollo* 7 becomes the first manned Apollo spacecraft launched into space.

In December, *Apollo* 8 becomes the first manned spacecraft to orbit the moon.

1969   *Apollo 11* astronaut Neil Armstrong becomes the first man to walk on moon.

1970   NASA launches *Apollo 13* on April 11.

On April 13, *Apollo 13*'s oxygen tank two explodes, threatening the ship's power and oxygen supply.

The *Apollo 13* crew improvises an air filter on April 15.

On April 17, *Apollo 13*'s command module *Odyssey* splashes down in the Pacific Ocean.

American Moments

FAST FACTS

Although the Apollo 13 mission did not land on the moon as planned, some experiments were completed. The Apollo 13 contributed to a study of launch phase electrical charge and successfully photographed Earth for a cloud study. It also sent part of its Saturn V launch rocket on a crash course with the moon for another experiment that was started during the Apollo 12 mission.

Odyssey, the *Apollo 13* command module, was originally displayed at the Musée de l'Air et de l'Espace in Paris, France. It was later moved to the Kansas Cosmosphere and Space Center in Hutchinson, Kansas.

As astronauts, James A. Lovell, John L. Swigert Jr., and Fred W. Haise Jr. logged many hours in space. Haise and Swigert logged 142 hours and 52 minutes each. Lovell, who logged 715 hours and 5 minutes, held the record for most time in space until the Skylab missions.

Swigert was elected to the U.S. House of Representatives in November 1982. However, he died before he could begin to serve his term.

The movie *Apollo 13* came to theaters in 1995. Its script was based on a book about the Apollo 13 mission by Lovell and Jeffrey Kluger. In the movie, Tom Hanks played Lovell.

WEB SITES
WWW.ABDOPUB.COM

Would you like to learn more about Apollo 13? Please visit **www.abdopub.com** to find up-to-date Web site links about Apollo 13 and other American moments. These links are routinely monitored and updated to provide the most current information available.

The crew of the Apollo 13 mission step aboard the USS Iwo Jima following splashdown in the Pacific Ocean.

GLOSSARY

acceleration: an increase in speed.

assassinate: to murder a very important person, usually for political reasons.

capsule: a pressurized compartment that can detach from a larger craft.

condensation: water from the air that becomes liquid because of a decrease in temperature.

cosmonaut: an astronaut from Russia.

dehydration: unusual loss of water from the body. This can be caused by an illness or by not drinking enough fluids.

far-ultraviolet: the part of the ultraviolet spectrum that has the shortest wavelengths. These wavelengths are between 100 and 300 nanometers.

flammable: easily set on fire.

fuel cell: a device that uses chemical reactions to produce electricity.

jettison: to discard or expel unwanted material from a ship.

nebulae: clouds of dust or gas in space.

nuclear: of or relating to the energy created when atoms are divided or combined.

pressurize: to maintain a normal atmospheric pressure during spaceflight.

rendezvous: a maneuver in which spacecraft approach each other in space.

spectrum: a range of characteristics of waves that can be charted.

Jim Lovell holds the American flag during a training exercise prior to the Apollo 13 mission.

thermostat: a device that regulates temperature.

trajectory: the path that an object takes through space.

ultraviolet: invisible waves of radiation that have a shorter wavelength than visible light, but a longer wavelength than X rays. Ultraviolet radiation goes outside the visible light spectrum at the violet end.**trajectory:** the path

World War II: from 1939 to 1945, fought in Europe, Asia, and Africa. Great Britain, France, the United States, the Soviet Union, and their allies were on one side. Germany, Italy, Japan, and their allies were on the other side.

INDEX